AN IMAGINATION LIBRARY SERIES

Colors of the Sea

CORAL REEF SURVIVAL

Eric Ethan and Marie Bearanger

Gareth Stevens Publishing
MILWAUKEE

For a free color catalog describing Gareth Stevens Publishing's list of high-quality books and multimedia programs, call 1-800-542-2595 (USA) or 1-800-461-9120 (Canada). Gareth Stevens Publishing's Fax: (414) 225-0377.
See our catalog, too, on the World Wide Web: http://gsinc.com

Library of Congress Cataloging-in-Publication Data

Ethan, Eric.
    Coral reef survival / Eric Ethan and Marie Bearanger.
      p. cm. — (Colors of the sea)
    Includes index.
    Summary: Examines some of the protective methods, such as camouflage, regenerating parts of their bodies, and traveling in schools, used by creatures living near coral reefs.
     ISBN 0-8368-1736-2 (lib. bdg.)
     1. Coral reef fishes—Behavior—Juvenile literature. 2. Coral reef ecology—Juvenile literature. 3. Camouflage (Biology)—Juvenile literature. 4. Animal defenses—Juvenile literature. [1. Coral reef animals. 2. Animal defenses. 3. Coral reef ecology. 4. Ecology.] I. Bearanger, Marie. II. Title.
III. Series: Ethan, Eric. Colors of the sea.
QL620.45.E84   1997
597.177'89—dc21   96-47569

First published in North America in 1997 by
Gareth Stevens Publishing
1555 North RiverCenter Drive, Suite 201
Milwaukee, WI 53212 USA

This edition © 1997 by Gareth Stevens, Inc. Adapted from *Colors of the Sea* © 1992 by Elliott & Clark Publishing, Inc., Washington, D.C. Text by Owen Andrews. Photographs © 1992 by W. Gregory Brown. Additional end matter © 1997 by Gareth Stevens, Inc.

Text: Eric Ethan, Marie Bearanger
Page layout: Eric Ethan, Helene Feider
Cover design: Helene Feider
Series design: Shari Tikus

The publisher wishes to acknowledge the encouragement and support of Glen Fitzgerald.

Printed in the United States of America

1 2 3 4 5 6 7 8 9 01 00 99 98 97

TABLE OF CONTENTS

Survival Strategies 4

What Is Camouflage? 6

How Do Fish Change Colors? 10

Why Are Some Fish So Visible? . . . 14

Escape! 18

Why Do Fish Form Schools? 20

Glossary 23

Web Sites 23

Places to Write 24

Index 24

SURVIVAL STRATEGIES

Coral reefs are home to various kinds of **predators**. This is because there are sea creatures on which the predators feed near the reefs.

To avoid being eaten by predators, some sea creatures hide in the coral. Others have the ability to make themselves hard to see even though they are in the open. A few fish are **poisonous** so predators avoid eating them. Some sea creatures survive even after a predator has eaten part of them.

These ways of avoiding predators are called survival strategies.

Barracuda, *Sphyraena*, are among the most feared of the reef predators.

WHAT IS CAMOUFLAGE?

A good way for some **prey** animals to avoid being eaten is through **camouflage**. These animals are able to disguise themselves. For instance, many fish can blend into their surroundings or can look like other objects.

The seafan goby is a naturally red fish that blends into its surroundings. It is camouflaged from predators when it keeps still near certain kinds of red coral.

A seafan goby, *Bryaninops*, is well camouflaged near red coral.

The longlure frogfish can also camouflage itself. It has blotchy colors that make its shape hard to recognize. **Algae** grow on its **scales** making it look even less like a fish.

To disguise itself, one type of hermit crab sticks bits of sponge onto its shell. Another type of hermit crab puts small sea anemones on its shell. The stinging **tentacles** of the anemones protect the crab as well as camouflage it.

The longlure frogfish, *Antennarius multiocellatus*, can barely be seen in the reef. It uses a small lure on its nose to attract prey.

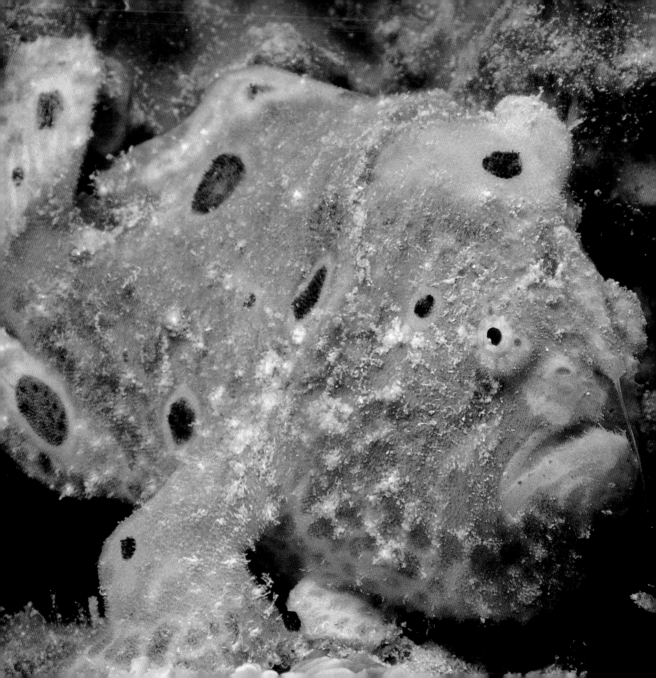

HOW DO FISH CHANGE COLORS?

Some fish are born with the colors necessary to be camouflaged in coral reefs. Other fish can change their colors to match their surroundings.

These fish are able to change colors because of special **chemicals** in their skin. The fish can control the chemicals to change their skin color quickly or slowly. The scorpionfish can change colors. This helps it hide while waiting to ambush prey.

The scorpionfish, *Scorpaenopsis*, is beautifully colored, but it is deadly to prey and predators. Its spines are poisonous.

Some fish can change their color and their **gender**. For example, female purple-blotched basslets are born with bright yellow scales. They swim in a group under an adult male. When the adult male dies, a leading yellow female replaces this fish, taking on the purple coloring and becoming male.

Bright red groupers flash a different color to make **parasites** stand out on their bodies. This helps fish called cleaning wrasses find the parasites and pull them off the groupers.

A female purple-blotched basslet, *Anthias pleurotania*, is born with yellow scales. As an adult, a leading female becomes purple and male.

WHY ARE SOME FISH SO VISIBLE?

Although some sea creatures near coral reefs try to hide, some do their best to be seen. This is useful to some **species**. Most cleaning wrasses have bright stripes on their sides. Marine scientists think the stripes help other fish identify the wrasses. This allows cleaning wrasses to get close enough to other fish to pull parasites from them.

But scientists have not discovered the purpose for the bright colors and patterns of many other fish.

The brightly colored blue tang, *Acanthurus coeruleus*, lives among the sponges and corals of the Caribbean.

At depths to about 30 feet (9 meters), sunlight makes the brilliant colors of fish easy to see. Just below this, colors begin to fade. At 60 feet (18 m) deep, all colors look black. The sea creatures in this book that live in deep water look colorful because strong flashlights were used to take the photographs.

Many deep-sea creatures have very bright colors. But without sunlight or artificial light from flashlights, they seem to have just black-and-white patterns. Why these sea creatures are so brightly colored when the colors cannot be seen is a mystery.

The longfin bannerfish, *Heniochus acuminatus*, is brightly colored and patterned. These fish form pairs for life.

ESCAPE!

Even the best camouflage does not fool predators all the time. Some sea animals do get caught, but a few of them are still able to escape.

The brittle star can move very quickly if a predator comes after it. If it is caught, however, it may still have a chance. If the predator bites off one of its legs, the brittle star can escape. Later, it will grow a new leg to replace the lost one. Some starfish can regrow an entire body and legs from a single leg and part of its central **disk**.

The brittle star, *Ophiothrix purpurea*, is well hidden against the coral reef.

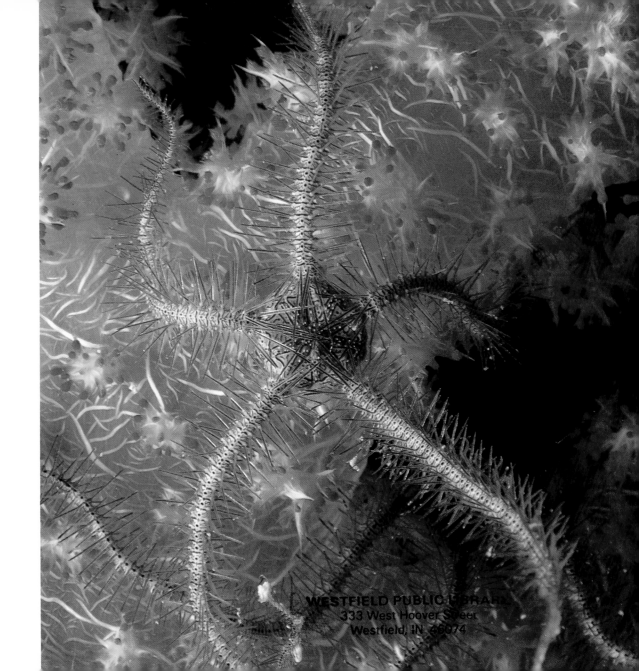

WHY DO FISH FORM SCHOOLS?

In order for a predator to catch prey, it usually has to see the prey. This gives the predator a clear target. So some fish form what are known as schools and swim as a group. To a predator, the schools appear to be a big, swirling cloud. This makes it difficult for the predator to see a single victim and go after it.

Even fish that are dangerous predators will "school" if they are threatened. Barracuda are fierce coral reef predators that are 24-35 inches (60-90 centimeters) long. But they will form large schools when the even mightier sharks or dogtooth tunas are nearby.

Schooling fish like these glassfish, *Parapriacanthus guentheri*, have many eyes looking out for predators.

Schooling fish, even in groups of hundreds, swim as though they are a single fish. They have nearly perfect **coordination**. To human observers, there are no obvious signals among the fish indicating when to turn or go up or down. But somehow, the fish all manage to move in the same way at the same time.

Schooling fish are a wonderful **symbol** for life on the coral reef. Each of the various sea creatures on the reef has a role to play that affects all the other creatures around it. The creatures live together in harmony and balance.

GLOSSARY

algae (AL-jee) — Water plants that are food for many sea creatures.

camouflage (KAM-o-flahzh) — Shapes or colors on an animal's body that disguise the animal and help it hide.

chemical (KEM-i-kuhl) — A substance that changes when mixed with another substance.

coordination (ko-or-deh-NA-shun) — The process of acting together in a smooth, steady way.

disk (DISK) — In this book, the round, flat center of a starfish's body.

gender (JEN-der) — A term that indicates whether an organism is male or female.

parasite (PAIR-ah-site) — A living being that attaches itself to and feeds off another living being to survive.

poisonous (POY-zeh-nus) — Having a substance that can injure or kill.

predator (PRED-uh-ter) — An animal that lives by feeding on other animals.

prey (PRAY) — An animal hunted by other animals for food.

scale (SKALE) — A small, thin, flat, hard plate that, in large numbers, forms a protective covering on the outside of some fish or other animals.

species (SPEE-sheez) — A group of living beings that are alike in certain ways.

symbol (SYM-buhl) — An object that represents or stands for another object.

tentacle (TENT-ah-cuhl) — A flexible, tubelike arm of a sea creature that is used for collecting food, holding, moving, or stinging.

WEB SITES

http://www.blacktop.com/coralforest/

http://planet-hawaii.com/sos/coralreef.html

PLACES TO WRITE

The Cousteau Society, Inc.
870 Greenbrier Circle, Suite 402
Chesapeake, VA 23320

Environmental Protection Agency
Oceans and Coastal Protection Division
401 M Street SW
Washington, D.C. 20460

Greenpeace (USA)
1436 U Street NW
Washington, D.C. 20009

Greenpeace (Canada)
2623 West Fourth Avenue
Vancouver, British Columbia V6K 1P8

Greenpeace Foundation
185 Spadina Avenue, Sixth Floor
Toronto, Ontario M5T 2C6

Center for Marine Conservation
1725 DeSales Street, Suite 500
Washington, D.C. 20036

National Geographic Society
17th and M Streets NW
Washington, D.C. 20036

INDEX

algae 8

barracuda 4-5, 20
blue tang 14-15
brittle star 18-19

camouflage 6-7, 8-9, 10, 18
chemicals 10
cleaning wrasses 12, 14
crabs 8

gender 12-13
glassfish 20-21

longfin bannerfish 16-17

longlure frogfish 8-9

parasites 12, 14
predators 4-5, 6, 10-11, 18, 20-21
prey 6, 8-9, 10-11, 20
purple-blotched basslets 12-13

scales 8, 12-13
schools 20-21, 22
scorpionfish 10-11
sea anemones 8
seafan goby 6-7

tentacles 8